# DAY OF THE DEAD

**Katie Donovan** was born in 1962, and spent her early youth on a farm in Co. Wexford. She studied at Trinity College Dublin and at the University of California at Berkeley, and spent a year teaching English in Hungary. She now lives in Dublin where she works as a journalist with the *Irish Times*. She has published three collections, *Watermelon Man* (1993), *Entering the Mare* (1997) and *Day of the Dead* (2002), all from Bloodaxe.

She is the author of *Irish Women Writers: Marginalised by Whom?* (Raven Arts Press, 1988), and has co-edited two anthologies: *Ireland's Women: Writings Past and Present* (with A. Norman Jeffares and Brendan Kennelly), published by Kyle Cathie (Britain), by Gill & Macmillan (Ireland) in 1994, and by Norton & Norton (USA) in 1996; and *Dublines* (with Brendan Kennelly), published by Bloodaxe in 1996.

KATIE DONOVAN

# *Day of the Dead*

BLOODAXE BOOKS

ISBN: 1 85224 592 1

First published 2002 by
Bloodaxe Books Ltd,
Highgreen,
Tarset,
Northumberland NE48 1RP.

www.bloodaxebooks.com
For further information about Bloodaxe titles
please visit our website or write to
the above address for a catalogue.

Bloodaxe Books Ltd acknowledges
the financial assistance of Northern Arts.

northern
arts

Cover printing by J. Thomson Colour Printers Ltd, Glasgow.

Printed in Great Britain by
Cromwell Press Ltd, Trowbridge, Wiltshire.

*for Stephen*

# Acknowledgements

Acknowledgements are due to the editors of the following publications in which some of these poems first appeared: *The Edgeworth Papers* (VI), *Kestrel, Poetry Ireland Review, The Recorder, Verse, The White Page/An Bhileog Bhán* (Salmon Publishing, 1999), *The Whoseday Book* (The Irish Hospice Foundation, 1999) and *WP Journal.*

Thanks are also due to the Arts Council of Ireland for a bursary which allowed me to take a sabbatical in 1999 to work on this book.

# Contents

# Day of the Dead, New Orleans

*(for Lar Cassidy)*


You would have loved one last night
of the syncopated 'Funky Butt',
with Big Al rolling
his great, luscious voice
out of the massive black mountain
of his chest,
the boys lifting their silver trumpets,
the flush in their cheeks
going right up to their thinning hair,
while the tomcat on the piano
sends his hands a-jitter
for the 'Charleston Rag',
and the sweet molasses drummer
drops his long lashes
and shimmies his cymbal.

All the vaults in the graveyard
are rollicking their brollies
with the beat and swish,
twirl and flourish;
in the voodoo haunt on Bourbon Street,
the obeah woman's hair stands up
with the tongues of serpents,
the clay ladies open their legs
and little heads peek out;
even Christ on his crucifix
has all the time in the world
for dixie.

My tears roll
when I think of the freezing day
we tried to warm
with our drums and poetry,
when we laid you down,
and carried your jazzy hat away.

In this city
where your shadow
takes a closer walk,
grief brims
like the upside-down grin
of the Mississippi
with its sad, booming boats,
and I think of you
as a great craft
powering down the current,

until your light failed
and you ran aground,
and we stood on the shore
in our Mardi Gras masks,
watching you sink,
wringing our hands;

and in your big marshmallow
and sweet-potato voice you said:
'Laissez le bontemps roulez,
laissez le bontemps roulez.'

# Bird

The shiny magpie head
jabs, strains, lunges,
and the claws strike fast.
It seems like hours
before the pitiless beak
pierces fluttering prey
for the last time;
holds it up, limp-necked,
for a final shake, and flies away.

This is not
the calm chorus of May birds
I had hoped to show you;
it is too much like the slow,
deliberate torture
that time is for you now:
the relentless peck
of long solitary days;
the beak has almost
finished off your eyes,
the claws have clenched your bird back
to a scrawny hunch.
Your thin hands flutter
as the days close in,
the unforgiving head
looms harsh over you,
shadowing your shallow breath,
wearing down your tired heart,
severing the memory cord.

One day soon I'll find you,
limp-necked and thrown aside,
the horrid beak stilled and flown,
your feathers floating free;
your breast still warm,
with all the gentle song you gave,
that no croaking death could pierce,
and lifts me always
on your spreading wing.

# Cherry
*(for Phoebe)*

You saw him waiting
at the foot of the bed.
He was fresh and young,
his brown eyes searching.
The tips of his fingers
were squared and bruised,
and you guessed
his trade was wood.

He told you of the splendour
of the cherry,
her limbs remembered
in the wardrobe's
sheen and grain;
even the shavings,
and the leftover crusts
of her bark
transform a hearth
with blossomed scent.

You offered him your hand:
delicate and long,
carrying in its lineaments
all the deft work
of your brush,
the fatigue of holding on,
when your heart
had lost its grip.

He took you then,
and freed your roots,
grown tired in the earth.

He lifted you
into the full flower
of the moon,
your feet trailing petals
like snow.

When I woke
for the first morning
into a world
where your breath
no longer stirred,
I wept into the empty basin
of my grief,

but now I smile,
because of your release,
into the forest
of the stars

# Reading the Keen
*(for Sarah McKibben)*


You came to learn grief:
you read the keens
of the lost women,
you mapped the fate
of their urgent tongue.
It was all a sorting
and a shuffling,
like a pack of cards;
you built the piles
of matching suits.
Then a freak wave
came crashing down
on your patterning
of history and language:
death snapped your reason.

It was time
to throw away the books,
pull down all the cards,
enter the wave,
away from any ladder
of thought's design,
to lose your legs from under you,
let it break you,
let it knit you,
let it wash you,
let it chew and swallow and spit you;
let it weep out of you
the great salt of despair,
let it tear you,
and bear you
all over
again.

You came to learn grief:
the keen of another country,
another age; yet it was here
you found your own lament.

# Bookey's Bridge, The Harrow, Wexford, 1798

*(for John and Thomas Donovan)*

You can speak of bridges,
of burning and hanging,
of building again,
and meeting in the centre
to shake hands.

I'd rather speak
of triangles,
of how I always cut myself
on the arrow-tip

pushing for closure.

Freedom, fraternity,
and godfearing
noble notions,
brought the cousins
with their cohorts,
bristling to the bridge,

John:
the cuckold yeoman
shouting for blood;
Tom:
the frightened rebel
choking him off;

right there
the yeoman's heart
shot out;
the rebel's heart
turned to stone.

The others ran away
from that family spilling,
lest its red triangle
soak the foolhardy motley
of their battle flags.

# The Blood So Thin

Swathes of orange groves for sale,
the water garden grown over;
on the lake shore,
the alligators rise,
swishing their long tails.

You still dwell here,
with the ghost
of your movie star face,
remembering picnics and parties,
tennis on the lawn –
the score, love-all, a mockery –
your voice and clothes
a silken net of elegance,
your perfect hands
made for holding bowls of orchids.

The black maid serves dinner
through the shying lapses
of your conversation,
and I go to sleep dreaming
of the hourglass spider,
its poison tooth lurking
behind fragrant wood-panelling,
fattening
on the bones of your father
who made his own end.

In morning light,
I search the last
of your grandfather's estate –
the mossy groves, the rain tree –
seeking clues to his dark heart,
the fierce architect
of your drowned palace.

The heron's call
draws me back to the reedy shore,
and when on a sudden heel
of frustrated rage,
I turn away,
the beast makes a splashy lunge,
sawing up on waves
behind me –

and for one second
I feel the jaws
at my naked leg,
but when I look,
the ancient scales
have sunk to the mud,
and there's only a ripple,
a twitch in the water,
to suggest the snarl and bite,
the dragging off,
the appetite
that nurses itself
through decades,
and must rob from the sun
any heat it can get:

the blood so thin,
the teeth so long,
the grip
impossible to break,
if you let it
take you down.

# Clew Bay, Anew

Long blue mountains
sleep in the smudged grey
of summer twilight;
the shadow cup of the sea.

In a seven-year sigh
of making over,
I let you swim out from me,
and the grief dives off
like a freed porpoise,
like a gull
shunting
on a lifting breeze.

This lovely place
couldn't save you
in your last months,
as the sickness raged
and clotted in your gut.

But now it offers me
a threshold
you never saw,
and I leave off guilt,
like the unwanted attentions
of a spurned lover,

I take this prize
gratefully,
this summer night,
this second chance,

as the last of you
unlinks and scissors off
towards some new Atlantis:

far away,
and ringed with peace

# The Creep

This is the room where he went mad,
where she shot up, where
I cannot sleep in the crooked bed,
haunted by the leavings of the past.

I light the lamp, shocking my eyes wide
when I find the carpet alive:
cockroach antennae twirling
like cheerleaders with batons
hailing the night, foraging for debris
from months of lodgers
perched briefly, and then gone.

By the wardrobe
the flash of feelers climbs my coat,
burrows my slipper's fur;
the bolder ones negotiate
the drooping end of my quilt.
I fling them off, and hunch,
frozen, on guard,
as they beetle back
to reclaim lost ground.

I wait out the night.
I will not let them scavenge
the precious booty of my brain.

At dawn they shrink back,
and I gather myself,
shake out the lavender lace
of my party dress
in the blessèd sun.

I think of how we dwell
each in our own room,
keeping the creep
at one hand's length –

and some of us fail.

# Back on Smack

She's at the door, rattling,
and you clench, striving
for the strength to keep her out.
Your memory was of your bright,
fond boy, and the days when she
was his sweetheart. You forgot
that even then he was smoking it.
Since he died, she's gone on,
been married, her husband's now inside;
her children fostered out.
She's roaming now, feeding off
whoever takes her in.
She came to you –
her petal skin and big eyes
a reminder of the good times –
telling you she was ready
to pack it all in, just needed
a base to get herself steady.
It's been two weeks,
and she's stolen your cash,
your silver, your cards.
She goes out at night to score,
comes home in the wee hours,
waking you into fear.
Tonight's the last straw.
After she left, you put on the chain,
drank tea and smoked cigarettes –
you say eating makes you soft.

When the rattle comes
your dog bares her teeth,
willing you to keep out
the night thieves,
who have robbed you blind
and left you lonely,
with a packet of fags
and a bottle of gin –
and the house full
of pictures of him.

## Crash

For the last
six minutes,
she had the hope
sucked out of her,
as her craft changed
from a bird
to a stone,
and her ears were filled
with screaming.

It took three weeks
to find the remnants
of her body –
a jawbone,
a broken piece
of rib –
there was slim salvage
for her family
to claim.

Her heart and lungs
were blown away
and never found;
neither
were her feet.

# Song of the Half Breed

I was only half the man
her people wished for,
they suffered me
to please her.

I was bound
in the ropes of her hair:
she was fine-boned
as a fawn,
and trembling soft
in my arms.

She lifted me so high,
I had the strength
of a full-grown grizzly;
the spread of an eagle,
riding the wind.

After the white men
bled the best
of her tribe,
I led the way
to the cool grass
of the mountains,
where our young were born.

Full years, until the season
when I watched her
turn yellow and waxen.
The old women bathed her
like a doll.

I left our children
to seek the town –
all rough hewn wood
and fighting.
I don't know what
I thought I'd find there,
perhaps a sign

of my father's track,
but it was no different
from before:
shunning faces, refuge only
where the shadows
hid my looks.

A white woman
showed some kindness,
until her husband
came for me
with his drunken gang.

Now my crooked body
stiffens in the street.
Soon the tattered corpse
will be shovelled up
and buried, with the rest
of the town's cast-offs.

I wait, as always,
torn between two worlds,
hoping for one to come,
and claim my broken form.

In vain.

# News Photograph, Grozny, January 1995

The little dolls are covered
with smears of jam and flour,
their mouths slack,
as though left down
in a gingerbread house,
by children,
baking.

Past the muzzy grains
of black and white,
I see
the dolls are children,
covered with smears
of blood and dust,
their mouths slack
with crying,
left down
in a shelled house,
by adults,
fighting.

## Treasures

I enter the house, and right away
the chaos falls on my head
in a paralysing hood.
Walls – creviced in secret
webs of rot – are down,
leaving chunks of plaster,
broken teeth of brick.
Dust grows a brazen fur
across every item in the place.
Wires hang slack nooses
with errant light-switches
to clunk my forehead.
The loo remains, lone throne
in the jags of drilled-up concrete.

I tiptoe up the stairs –
clogged with gobs
of plaster and cement –
through the grime
of the temporary kitchen,
and into the cave of the bedroom.

Out of my bag
I spill my treasures:
laundered sheets,
smelling warm and dry.
I climb into the heaven
of a clean bed,
my skin thrilling to the feel
of washed cotton.
I float in its embrace,
dreaming of the day
when I will soak in a hot bath
under my own sturdy roof;
dreaming of the night,
when bed will mean more
than a quick escape
from an avalanche
of dirt.

# Motherspell

Before we were born,
our mothers hatched the plot.
Lacing letters
across different worlds,
they laid the spell of our future,
as we fattened in their wombs.
Their will fuelled the hot surprise
of our teen encounter:
we wore the charmed inevitability
of our bodies joining
like invisible signatures.

Whether you were daring
the horns of Spanish bulls,
or confiscating cigarettes
from Roman urchins
to stub on your own wrists;
whether you were sending me
silver earrings from Brazil,
or settling down at home
with a sensible fiancée,
you stalked my horizon.
And I – whether high
on mushrooms in a Mexican glade,
or knocking the stones
of an old house into new shape;
whether testing my mettle
in pidgin Hungarian,
or resting in the arms
of a longtime lover –
I was cross-stitched on your skin
those years of other promises,
other lives.

Now we face each other,
tallying the lines,
resisting and revisiting,
summing our doubts; our desires.
At last, as though our mothers
were whispering the cues,
we cry out our need,
our lips seek the old haven,
and the spell settles heavier,
hobbling our footsteps
like broken wishbones.

# Airport

I couldn't let you go
without a kiss,
a kiss that opened
and grew, fizzed
and crackled
along my synapses,
left my mouth
aflame;

spun me back
sixteen years
to the feel
of a car bonnet
under my spine,
and you
pressing
me down,
all the stars
converging
in our lips
touching
for the first time;

spun me on
to now, and our
changed bodies,
our adult business,
our senseless yearning
for a child.

And then you were gone.

It was 7 a.m., a Sunday,
and I was left to wander
in the parking lot,
a familiar territory
whose signs
I could no longer read.

# Has Anybody Seen My Gal?
*(Toronto, September 1995)*

> *'Five foot blue, eyes of blue...*
> *Has anybody seen my gal?'*


I'm here
in the silver leaf shimmy
of birch; windstrung cloud,
lemon of aspen,
scarlet of maple,
skirts of sumac
crimsoning the roadside;
caught in the fall
of turning trees,
rows of fat pumpkins,
the crazy teeth
of Indian corn.

Here are the tunes
my mother sang to,
the yellowbrick house
of her girlhood,
gardens of black squirrels,
the church
where she made her vows;
and here is my own first love,
the sweet whirl of his mouth –
beckoning.

I fondle a string of dreamstones
on the bracelet of our past –
like when my hand,
fringed in velvet and lace,
first felt his touch,
and opened, a magic flower
in the dark –
the old songs haunt their claim
one more time,
before I slip the clasp
and let them go.

# Going Under

Today you're swelled
with boasts of air,
lifting a bright fiction
into the sun.

I smile
and go up with you:
the story you make is for me –
I am the most beautiful princess
the world has ever seen,
my brilliance is as limitless
as the vast landscape
spreading beneath us;
I am the jewel at the centre
of a dull, unknowing world,
and you have fashioned for me
a gorgeous setting.

But tomorrow
you'll split the ground
from underneath my feet,
drag me down to a dark stage,
where you're the puppet master,
the lonely punisher.
You'll bind me to the chains
of your painted cavalcade,
hurrying us into masks and costumes,
with you the blameless hero,
I the maddened queen.

I'll peel the guilt-rind
of the pomegranate
you push upon me,
trying to remember
my own seed plot,
back in the ordinary world
where I know myself:
what I have done,
what I have not done.

I'll ask you to come
to the level
between the ether
and the doom,
to my fields of grass
and simple blossom –
you will not even
look at me.

I'll find the strength
to throw the acid
pomegranate pulp
into the cinder
of your imaginings,

and as I leave, I'll say:
'Let its fossil fruit
be your comfort now.'

## Your Want

I feel your want
poking my skirt:
an insistent dog
that will not be cuffed away.
Even as I swoon to sleep,
I know you are disappointed,
your want unslaked.

Mornings I am strung
on the taut bow
of your expectation:
the bed
is a quiver of arrows.

Your want puts me in a sweat
with the need to get free:
it sends any want of mine
on the run.

If I could just
have the space
to dally
through the garden
of myself,
and find my want
all in leaf and bloom,
I would pluck a bouquet
and bring it to you,
moist with fresh dew
like me for you.

## The Bed

Today I strip the bed –
like pulling off a skin –
the bare mattress
is a quilted map
of places we never reached.

I twist out
the long screws
that bolt the frame together.
The bed falls apart –
a loose rack of bones.

It was a stormy night
when we first fetched up here,
you ferrying me and the furniture
to a last stop
before you flew off.

You fixed the bed together
so you could leave guilt-free,
knowing I had a place to sleep
among the chaos and debris.

Six years your handiwork
stayed put, me in it,
testing other loves,
or warming my own span.

After this dismantling
I feel like a prisoner
with the shackle off,

my flesh tender
from the familiar grip
I'd forgotten
I was wearing.

# My Cassandra

Long after your clumsy flight,
I chance upon a cache
of your belongings
you never bothered
to relieve me of.
I thought I'd weighed
the laughing best of us
alongside your treachery
and found a balance;
found a guilty place in me
that froze you to adultery,
forced you to lie later,
impaling my sanity –
a bewildered beast –
on barbed wire.

But now I swallow
broken glass again.
I open a stash
of copperplate letters:
a pile of lover's notes
full of whimsical quotes,
and dashes of French,
from 'Rosie', lusting for you.
The date? Only half-way through
our misbegotten stretch,
the spring we holidayed –
coincidentally – in Brittany,
frolicking under menhirs,
building in the sand.

I hold my body – captive
of an unfinished war –
whose pangs I shushed and shunned,
whom I recognise
as my Cassandra,
calling out to me in a voice
I am only really hearing
now.

# Miss Havisham Heart

Famished,
I open her rusted lock
and tug her musty wedding-dress –
it tears in my hand,
with a papery sigh
of dust and old lint.
She is in a trance,
her eyes fixed
on the empty chair beside her.
In her arms she rocks
the phantom child of her grief,
grown fat with the years
she has lavished
on its nourishment,
offering her breast of sour milk,
spooning in the uneaten wedding cake
of her mouldering hopes.

I show her the open door:
the groom stands outside,
his golden hair alight in the sun:
he has come for her at last.
But she will not stir,
no matter how I tell her
that with one touch
of his beautiful hand,
she will be beautiful too.

She does not believe.
She does not believe.

Somewhere in the cellar,
a girl is crying:
'Let me out, I will go to him.'
But no one hears her plea.

After all, that is a chamber
Miss Havisham sealed up
many years ago.

# Motherlode

*(Ballynahinch, Co. Galway)*


Waking, sheetswaddled
in the linen field of the bed,
we pleasure our vision
with scarlet geraniums
leaning from the windowsill
to tease the flint head
of the mountain,
capped in the rich blue
of an Indian summer morning.

We are drawn to the silver curve
of pine-flanked river,
fairy pink dart of flower.

Here is your hatching ground:
a motherlode of peat,
of square turrets
in white light and heather.
As the wind sways
her purple-tufted grasses,
she throws her beauty
like a gorgeous scarf
over a perfect shoulder,
and you, mesmerised again, rise
to follow and feed; to sink
in the lull of land water,
the flop of fish,
the cradle of mosses and maidenhair
spreading out of impossible stone.

I imagine it is her, too,
whose fingernails of rain
on my shrinking skin
hasten my solitary way,
across the dwindling landscape
back to the swarming claims
of my week's routine.

Nightfall, and our voices
strum across telegraph wires
necklacing the land.
I can hear the hollow heart of you,
as you tell of sweetening the dark
with the blackberries you gathered,
simmering for jam.

The fragrance mocks you,
like your mother
saying goodbye to her son,
jewelled and perfumed,
as she turns out your light,
and leaves you for some party
of her own.

# Coral

I buy you coral:
white, floral,
the one lure
in the giftshop
that shines pure.

Why did the coral
call me to its shelf?
It is all I want to be:
beautiful, unspoilt,
itself.

There's more:
its harsh pores – that sing
when your fingers lightly play –
suggest the hidden thing in me
that will not bend,
that cuts you
if you press too close,

and, if it's rattled,
breaks in jagged brittles,
waiting to needle you
in the dark.

# Honey and Salt

For a week
I have been full
of nothing but salt.
Lot's wife to the 'T',
I've been looking back
over our season
of trysts and calls,
poisoning myself
on salt.

This morning I wake
to a glaze of gold:
the wind sends drops
sliding off leaves
like honey
off a knife,
and I am spreading
sweet scarlet sap.

After so much salt,
this honey
is wrung from me
at some cost.
My belly is like
a scoured pot,
pitted and sore,
wary
of new concoctions.

# Puffer Fish

*(In Japan the puffer fish is a delicacy,*
*but parts of the fish are poisonous, so*
*it must be prepared with great care)*

You will not claim
the most delicious prize:
you fear the knife
has not filleted out
the poison.

You sniff:
distrustful.

Strange and crude
that the source
of your hope and worry
should be fleshed
in one glittering scoop.

You cast it away,
take to the wind,
preferring the phantoms
of the clouds;

their insubstantial fare
is cleaner to your palate,
than the pouting lips
that beckon you
to sit and eat.

# Rival

Let me attempt to explain
how I aroused in you
such perfunctory passion:
there was someone else, who
was darker, closer, harder,
and opened up your dream
of fraught, forbidden ardour,
a cause you could believe in.
My body spread and waiting
was not the meal you craved,
you nibbled, fiddled, taking
with bored smugness what I gave,
and all the while your thoughts
were conjuring a scene,
where he was secret lover
and you were his glad queen.
His rough beard, your hairless skin
naked beneath his hands,
his sex, a heavy, rising fin
lifting you to different lands;
to the thrilling violence of his world
and the weapons he has hurled,
this handsome, grizzled, action man
is in your bed and in command.
He is your own lost other side
now stiff with lust and stiff with pride.
You open your eyes, but there's only me –
you're disappointed, naturally –
you wanted the press of manly thighs,
you'd swop my woman's mess of fruit
for the virile scent of gelignite,
you're getting hard at the thought of him,
but you're stuck with me, so you begin
to wriggle free, waxing maudlin.

Let's drop the farce,
I have no dart to strike your heart
and enter your sleek shapely arse.

# Rocks

We found, dropped
like a fruit from the sky:
a hunk of granite, dazzling
in its apricot encrustations
among the limestone slabs.
Afterwards I remember
not the long blur of stone,
but that singular,
crystalline shine
of radiant granite;

just as when I weigh
our time together,
I realise how my mind
sifted out the sheets of grey,
to feast on irregular treasures –
the light in your blue green eyes;
the sudden serendipities
in your casual remarks;
the magnet of your hand
on mine –

and not the many hours
when you were as dark to me
as a coffin rock,
until the time came
when you crept
into a stone chamber
and disappeared,
leaving me
with flecks of mica
on my skin,
memories of ignition
when you shone like a comet,

before the lava
of your heart
died back
to its native element.

## Sunset

In the pink embrace
of the icy sunset,
the hills arching
their dark backs
to a last blue
and peach caress,
we marvelled
at the lingering
golden-tinged evening,
how it lit up the sea;
the red boats.

In that final
illumination
we let each other go,
our hearts sinking
like the exhausted sun,
after the orchestra
of light.

# Island

I dreamed I was an island
of trees and spiderwebs,
and hummingbirds
trembling in my hair.

You found my shore
ready at last to say goodbye.
Our farewell was sleepysoft
and final, not the horror
of broken nights refiguring
our fractured past.

But knowing your laughing,
trickster ways,
I pushed you off
even as you kissed –
if I let you stay too long,
you'd quickly twist the throats
of all my little birds.

You did not press,
but when you left,
I found a scared
half-strangled body
in a tangle of my hair.
You had tried to pinch
one bird, and failed.

I took the panting creature
in my hand, and watched
the beak begin to calm,
the wings relax
their dull and frozen hunch.
The neck perked up,
the tiny claws had life again
to join the nesting flock
behind my ear.

Exhausted by your visit,
I rested in the crooning,
busying life of the birds,
the burgeoning leaves,
and spiders at their craft;

my spine and ribs
an oratory,
where my heart could grow.

## Meet Me in the Palace

The prince will meet me
in the Palace,
and in his kiss
I'll wake
from a trance of years:

I'll be grumpy
with sleepdust,
and smarting
with the woken pain
of scars;

I'll fight
against the slippage
as I lose ground,
as I lose the box
I've grown into
like a home.

Still, he'll not fail me
in the Palace,
and in his kiss
the numb years
will spill down
my shoulders;

till I step
from my dark habit:
new as milk,
and shining
in my crown.

## Don't Look Back

It will take long hours
to coax her song:
you must follow
the fault-line down
through rock
and crabbed roots.

Carry your gift to her.
A lifted trophy,
it ripples and plumbs
and strokes; it will comb out
her tangles.

If you let her,
she will follow your note
up through the stone years,
the heavy press
of choked down clay,
the dried-up
riverbed.

Her throat will open
to the singing
of a full kettle
searing the house.

Just don't look back,
until you've won
the light.

# Prayer of the Wanderer
*(to Brigit)*


Racoons shriek
and alligators creep
beneath my window.

Trees are lapped
by waterlog,
their arms bearded
with the tangled grey
of Spanish moss.

My hands
are wrinkled
and lost.

I wish for a mooncow
to carry me home
to the land of apples.

I would lure her
to my house
with sweet grass.
I would press my face
against her fragrant belly,
and try for milk.

I have left her sign
of woven rushes
over my door,
while I roam this place
of swamps and broken shells.

I pray she keeps all safe
till my return:

let my house not be fallen,
nor eaten in flame,
let my loved ones flourish,
and my garden thrive.

One glimpse
of the white star
on her great head
would give me peace.

Even her hoofprint
in the night sky
would tell of home.

# Lost in Fjaerland

*(Nesehaugen mountain, Sognefjord, Norway)*


Blue crystals crown the valley,
spilling an apron of ice
with a subterranean churn
of glacier milk,
feeding the green sway
of the freezing fjord.

On the sheltered floor:
windless meadows of buttercup,
the hot smell of cattle
in the grass.

I'm halfway up the mountain,
air clean on the tongue,
a cuckoo in the pines,
rollmop of fern,
red lichen on grey stone,
the rush and sliver
of water melting down.

At the top – wrong-footed
by sudden drifts of resilient snow –
I'm lost, alone, surrounded by sun,
brilliant on white peaks:
an insect in a blind desert.

I squelch back without a path,
ears tuned for the gush
of the waterfall,
hands and legs scrubbed raw
by needles of dwarf scrub,
stymied by a sheer drop
of rock.

I am hours scrambling in footholds,
a wailing wreck stumbling
over rotting wood, scree,
sodden moss, clouts of snow,

heart-stopping steeps of granite.
Small clefts offer violets,
heathers, the delicate bells
of white flowers.
I fumble on:
sore, torn, bruised and wet,
dragging my fears behind me
like a skeleton.

Sounds of sheep bells
and wagging lambs give me joy,
their brown pellets
leading to something
that might be a path;

then, the breakthrough
when I find a shallow way
to a slope of sapling birch,
a sunny shelf, where I sink
into dry grass, my bones melting
out of the claw of cold,
watching a black spider
leg it through the blades;
above, a red squirrel
balancing on a branch.

The creatures mock me,
at home here, while I am at sea,
my eyes averted from walls of rock,
the chilly torrents crushing down,
the fields and tops of ice.

# May

I pass
the low granite wall
hung with green,
and scan the branches
for signs.
It's the urgent calling
from fledgling beaks
that sends me looking;

but there's no cup of moss
hidden in the tree.
The little shrills
are lower.

I put my eye
to the cracked masonry
and see the tiny tufts,
pulsing their cries.

Bright caps and black eyes
crowd towards the light,
clamouring to be fed.

All night I dream
of hollow stone
full of feathers,
of a rock
that sings

## Elektra

Like a salmon
swimming blind
from half-way
round the world,
under the heels of waves
into the crowded mouth
of the estuary,
against a white
river current,
and on up
to the birth pocket
of a hill stream;

so I ride
the massive wheels
of the train,
past flooded fields
and wet woods
breathing mist,
in a haze of lost sleep
and sudden sunshafts,
until my feet
touch the platform,
and my eyes find
your waiting face,
fleshing the source
of all my wanderings.

# Evensong, Rocky Mountain National Park

Sun peers
over the icy shoulder
of flat-top mountain:
across the meadow
elk move in evening light.
Long ears twitch
as they stoop to graze,
the furry discs
of cream-coloured rumps
rolling in unison.

Crickets chorus
in the marshy grass,
the creek tumbles and turns,
dark melt waters rushing down;
a bird calls from the pines
in a shower of musical drops.

Coyote
comes out of the trees,
and makes ready to sing.
He opens his white throat
to the clouds,
a long howl swoops
from dark lips
drawn back over pointed teeth.

In the backwash
of the echo,
an answering call
travels on the air.
Ears cocked,
coyote trots to the road,
turns his head
to watch for tourist cars,
and crosses
to the trees beyond
following the song
into the twilight.

# The Crossing

Lurched in the smack
of steep waves,
soaked in spray,
no fixed star
to comfort the eye,
but a thick night
of pitch and toss,
and me clenching
in numb spasms
of heave and spew.

The kind hand
of the ferryman
pulled me through,
a shivering, dizzy
unsteady wreck,
my limbs astray,
my fingers blue.

On the island,
the heat
of a good fire
dried the salt
from my skin,
and your face
came swimming
down the long table
washed in candlelight.

You led me
into a new night
of moonwink sky,
and a glimmering bird
wading
in the harbour shallows.

A drink-happy sailor
lifted us
up the stone roads

in his rusted craft,
chortling at the wheel –
we sprawled,
laugh-nuzzling
with every rut and bounce.

In the sleeping house,
we made our retreat
to the tide
of thigh and tongue,
and melting tip;
your hands gentle
under my sway,
your blonde chest
a warm harvest
as we fell down
the white water,
till we drowned together –
a tangle of driftwood
in the tiny bed.

After the hours
of knowing,
came the morning
of not saying,
so, stepping on the ferry,
I flung a last smile
across the deck,
it fell into the pale net
of your goodbye face,

and then the waves took me
in a calm swelling day
back to shore.

## La Nageuse

*(for Sinéad, inspired by a figurine in the Egyptian collection at the Louvre)*

Her big black eyes,
and Cleopatra hair
were elegance itself;
her body a lovely line.
I thought she was
a trowel for flour,
until you said
the swimming girl
was proffering a spoon
of powder,
her little wooden feet
raised up to paddle
in the stream,
her long brown arms balancing
the duck-shaped vessel,
fitted with folding wings
to keep her cargo dry.

She swam towards me,
bearing her ancient wares.
I felt a shifting in my breast
like the opening of wings;
my face tilted,
composing itself
for powdering
out of some past
that flits in memory
like a wavering reed.

Perhaps I was ready –
after years of a bare face –
for the gift of the duck spoon,
a ceremony centuries old.

She offered me the princess
I once dressed myself up
to be.

# Dip

Scuff down sandy steps,
arches stipple and sink
on crunchy damp stones;
shell rims.
Toes, naked pink
lead the wade,
skin gasping,
going down
into grey-green
thick of salt,
shiver of wave-tip
on thigh, belly,
breast,
up to the chin,
hair-ends
ribboning,
white arms
marked
with the cling
of magenta fronds.

Eyes rove
to whale hump
of mountain;
pink and yellow
of shore blossom;
the island
goldening up
out of the mirrorball bay.

My playbody
needs no virtual reality,
only this
late summer dip
in the sea.

## Skiing on Water

The silver surface of the bay
pinkens in the mountains'
folded rose,
the evening warm
as a loving cup
into which I fall
like a cartoon big foot,
my hands reaching
for the bar of the boat,
body crouched and braced
for the sudden pull,
the quiver in the knees,
then the miraculous
up;

water breaking
beneath my skim,
the motor song
of the boat pulling me on
in a zoom current,
through mountain and sunset,
over the sheen of the sea,
scudding and splashing
beneath my swoop.

I bend to the leap of spray,
then rise again
in the fleet throb,
hair flung back,
face split open
in a whoop of glee,

till the flight swooshes slow,
and I drop off
like a fattened bee,
helpless and heavy
from feeding on the wind,
shaking from the force
of what I have held.

## (k)Night

Day sinks
in a blaze
of hot coals.

Night spreads
his dark wing
over the valley.

He blows the dust
from the leaves
of the almond tree.

He soothes
the hot bellies
of the happy sheep.

His music
comforts my ear:
the neckbells

of the beasts, foraging;
the crickets'
warbling strings.

He sees me
leaning
from the tiled balcony.

His scented breath
softens
my sun-blasted skin.

He lifts up
his velvet hand
to offer me

a moonflower
quivering on the vine:
it unfolds

petal by veined petal
into a fragrant
star.

# Early

You loll in surf,
your curly chest
sparkling
with drops of brine.

A wave rolls in:
you throw back
your arms,
surrendering
on its white wing.

Laugh-shivering
I hold you:
unexpected treasure
from a wrecked cargo.

You touch your lips
to my brow;
lift my foot
to brush sand
from my fussy toes.

When we kiss
the sun rises
between my hips.

This
is courtship.

## Picnic

Green smell of crushed grass
as we sit and spread the food:
oily leaves of the vine,
fat beans' butter on the tongue,
crack of peppercorn; tart of olive,
the succulence of dates.

Late gold sun on our hair,
scented smears on our fingers,
and you full of memories
of gooseberries
in a boyhood garden.
Laughter rocks us in its chair
until I have to stop your mouth
with a kiss, savouring garlic;
almonds; the hum of wine.

How does the dizzy sandwich
find its way to the right place,
in the mortar and pestle
                    of our embrace?

## About Face

Your face is a mask
of hazel and olive
in the secret valley
of Gleannta an Easig,
fastened on the dark lake,
the purple scree,
the frozen fall.
Yield of ochre needles
at our feet,
tongue of shore sand,
lick of lichen
on toothy rock;
and me
with the silent pines
at my back,
remembering
the intimate rafters
of your room,
my hands finding warm flesh
under black silk,
your face
spread out beneath me
full of smiles
like a cat
in the sun.

# Yellow

I am the yellow
of the sunflower quilt
in whose petals
we lie;
the fall of early light
through curtains' buttercup;
the egg-yolk hearts
of open crocuses
on frosted grass;
the lemon-beaked daffodils,
stretching their long throats –
ready
to frill
and dance.

# What Men Are For

You plunge the nap
of your otter's head
down the quiver and pool
of my flesh:

you come up gasping,
with pearls between your teeth.

Your face to my breast,
belly, thigh,
you coax me
to pour out my scent.

I plant my lips
in the toasty furrows
and ruby globes
of your beckoning form.

All night I am clasped
to the deep earth of your chest.

My morning hips are full of you
as I lurch through traffic
in a taxi to the train;

my mouth, red with kisses,
smiles in the knowing:

you have written my number
on your hand.

## Him

He washes through my senses –
a lovely dye –
tinting me rose and peach,
tanging me pineapple,
like edible chunks of sun.

He stops the traffic
as he brings
my flowering wrist
to the press
of his lips;
his big boot
alongside
my lifting toes.

I quicken:
a burst of birds
on a blue sky.

He takes me
like a river
takes a stone;

or like the arrow
he flourishes and fits,

and lets
fly.

# A Breath of the Rose

*(Chapada dos Veadeiros, central Brazil)*


Lovely Luciano
leads me safely across the river,
up the rain slip path
past the spines of giant palms,
and the fist-sized spider
lurking by my foot,
to the Valley of the Moon
where I glide in rocky saucers
of dark water.

At night he brings me
to the forest pool:
we bob in humming darkness,
the tufted tops of trees
and shyblur stars our canopy.

Lovely Luciano
has a voice like honey:
when he says my name
it sounds like cake.
He has tawny eyes
that watch and weigh,
and a slender nape.

In his heart
he bears a rose
for the music of an Irish girl
he has never seen: Dolores,
a name he lingers over,
savours.

Lovely Luciano
makes me lemongrass tea
when my stomach goes on fire.

He left the millions in the city –
the filthy air and traffic snarls
and taximen with guns.
Now he lives a simple life,
eating pumpkin as the crickets fiddle,
lazy in the portal,
so much left behind.

# Portal

*(Chapada dos Veadeiros, central Brazil)*

Here are riches:
fat grass strewn with fairy glitter,
red dragonflies whisking in noon heat,
forest frogs serenading
our cradle loll
in the night of the hot spring.

Turbulent water pounds my flesh
in a head-drowning rush,
a pair of parrots haggle
in a clatter of red and blue feathers,
a green-tongued bootlace snake
circles in the apricot dust.

My toes splay on rock
to reach a ledge
beside a ton of water,
crashing on stone, spuming
rainbows down the gorge,
fern-lashed,
flashing with the metallic wings
of bird-sized butterflies.

Jasmine, mimosa, bougainvillaea –
my way is perfumed
with open-tongued blooms,
with the hot liquorice steam
of the hillside after rain.

I fly away
holding a keepsake from the garden –
a nest of clear quartz –
a drop spilled
from an upside down moon.

# Abadiania, Brazil

Enthralled
in the vision
of what may come,
the pilgrims wait,
garbed in white,
for the man to incarnate,
for the bloodletting,
the stitching,
the miracle.

For long hours,
I hover
in the heavy element
of the waiting.
I try my shapes
to force a happening.
There's the fist
I wield in the water
that hits nothing.
There's the float
as I let go and hope
I'll be carried through.
There's the voice I find
when pain trips me,
and the lovely face of a woman
who outwits the stone
in her breast,
whittling it daily
with blades of light.

She glides through
the morass of people
to bring me succour.
She leads me face to face
with the wide eyes
of the man,
who sees and contains
misery; agony;
the despair of the dying.

I'm a voiceless squeak
before the big bear
sonorous force of him.

One look is enough
to sum me up,
before he turns away
into the restless field
of his vision,
the spreading map
of need and disease
in which I am a mere dot.

I go past a room
of abandoned crutches,
past the paralysed man
who is laughing
because he can move his hands,
past the little girl
who is still dumb.

I am as empty
as the blue balcony
as full
as the white oleander,

one hand
swipes numb tears,
the other
spreads folds
of my gauzy skirt
like a parachute,
readying
for the lift

# Wow, João

He pulls through the tranced air
the hand of a volunteer
like a lion with a deer.
He flourishes his knife,
and scrapes the delicate gelatin
of the rolling eye.
He shoves surgical scissors
up the flared nostril
with a dextrous twist.
The head is pushed back,
gnarled and distorted
like a petrified tree.
In his grip, the scissors
delve and divine:
a miner sourcing gold.
A pull and flick,
and out they pop
in a fall of blood.

Spellbound,
the volunteer
is carried away,
borne in a chair
by swift-footed acolytes.
Blood from his nose
lies pooled on the floor.

The daze breaks
when the conjuror leaves,
taking his hypnotic hands
and regal face
to the wicker throne
in the white room.

We go into our lines
waiting for an audience,
we, the cautious ones
who do not wish for knives.

We ask him to work his art
with invisible stitches
and herbal potions;

to take our eyes
and gently tear away
the veil.

# Visit

He'll come tonight
like a Milky Bar version of Dracula,
white cloak winging his big body
all the way from Brazil.

He'll find me sleeping,
arrayed in bridal white
for his delectation.
Like a little girl on Christmas Eve,
I'm hardly able to close my eyes,
thinking of it.

He's already had his way
with my inside,
and this is the last
of his ministrations:
to unpick the stitches
after my invisible operation.

I want to see him –
the big, red-eyed face;
the broad chest
and strength of him –
at his work.

But I'll be asleep,
dreaming of the room
where airy fingers
snipped and sewed
my scarred belly,
and I cradled myself in a thrall
of fascination and fear.

I'll be dreaming
of the long journey
when, weak and weeping
with queasy post-op blues,
I could scarcely lift
my baggage home.

When I wake tomorrow,
will I find a big handprint
on my lily-whites?
a telltale scalpel dropped?

I still crave
a smidgeon of the tangible:
he leaves me puzzling, mystified,
unable to explain
the change.

# Confluence

Beneath the amber hood
of the street lamp,
beside the black gates
of the somnolent park,
we are eyed by fanlights,
flanked by motionless cars.

In this blind Georgian lane,
you lean in
to claim a kiss.

I offer you
my goodnight lips,
staying like a shut purse
in your embrace,
wary after years
of opening too fast,
my burns still hurt and proud.

Yet the sweetness of your mouth,
and your tongue – a luscious,
sinuous sea-creature –
is a feast I cannot resist;

nor can I pull back
from the strength in your arms
as you draw me close,
loosening your coat
to fold me
in your cinnamon heat.

Here it is, timeless,
a scene on a street:

a man and a woman
tongued and grooved
into one.

## Seasoned

When you find me
I am the late grape,
ripening
as the evening
is laced with frost,
and rot snuffles
in the splendour
of the leaves;

you are the chestnut,
polished; unsheathed,
ready
for the earth
to take him in,
for crested candles
in the spring.

# Far Away; Inside

When I leave you
the movement of my breath
lingers in your chest;
you say it is the way skaters
still sense the ground
singing in their soles
long after
hanging up their wheels.

When I sleep alone,
I am still the cello
your fingers feel for;
the pattern of your dreamplay
sings in my belly
like a signature.

Your absent hands
articulate their music
on my skin;
just as, far away,
the ghost of my breath
rises inside your ribs.

# Notes

**Day of the Dead:** New Orleans is well known as the jazz capital of the world. It is also a melting pot of cultures and religions, from the Irish to the French and the African, from Christianity to Voodoo. Funerals there are looked on as occassions for dancing and singing. 'Laissez le bontemps roulez' is New Orleans speak for 'Let the good times roll'. Lar Cassidy, arts administrator, jazz lover and pagan, had a New Orleans style funeral and I know would have fitted into that city with gusto.

**Bookey's Bridge:** This is a bridge at the Harrow, near Ferns, where the first confrontation of the 1798 rebellion took place between a group of yeomen and rebels. The conflict was at its most intense in Wexford, where some families, such as my own, took opposing sides.

**Song of the Half Breed:** My ancestry includes more than one Native Canadian forebear. During supervised past life regression I experienced the story told in the poem – vividly, and with enormous grief.

**Meet Me in the Palace:** The Palace is one of Dublin's oldest pubs.

**Prayer of the Wanderer:** Brigid is an Irish saint, originally a pagan goddess. She is the saint of poetry, protection (her cross in your house will prevent it from burning down) and fertility (her emblems include cows and apples).

**Abadiania, Brazil:** João Teixeira de Faria is a psychic healer who holds court in a remote Brazilian village. He gives "invisible" operations, prescribes herbs, and, without anaesthetic or sterilisation, uses a scalpel and other instruments on volunteers with a variety of ailments, including cancer.

**The Visit:** A week after an invisible operation, the patient is instructed to wear white and lie on a white bed that night, as João will come to unpick the stitches.